Please visit our website, www.enslow.com. For a free color catalog of all our high-quality books, call toll free 1-800-398-2504 or fax 1-877-980-4454.

Library of Congress Cataloging-in-Publication Data
Names: Walton, Kathryn, 1993- author.
Title: Visit the Midwest / Kathryn Walton.
Description: Buffalo, NY : Enslow Publishing, [2024] | Series: Visit America's regions! | Includes bibliographical references and index.
Identifiers: LCCN 2023033348 (print) | LCCN 2023033349 (ebook) | ISBN 9781978537514 (library binding) | ISBN 9781978537507 (paperback) | ISBN 9781978537521 (ebook)
Subjects: LCSH: Middle West–Description and travel–Juvenile literature.
Classification: LCC F351 .W29 2024 (print) | LCC F351 (ebook) | DDC 917.7–dc23/eng/20230803
LC record available at https://lccn.loc.gov/2023033348
LC ebook record available at https://lccn.loc.gov/2023033349

Published in 2024 by
Enslow Publishing
2544 Clinton Street
Buffalo, NY 14224

Copyright © 2024 Enslow Publishing

Portions of this work were originally authored by Kathleen Connors and published as *Let's Explore The Midwest*. All new material in this edition is authored by Kathryn Walton.

Designer: Claire Wrazin
Editor: Natalie Humphrey

Photo credits: Series art (leather spine and corners) nevodka/Shutterstock.com, (map) Karin Hildebrand Lau/Shutterstock.com, (stamped boxes) lynea/Shutterstock.com, (old paper) Siam SK/Shutterstock.com, (vintage photo frame) shyshak roman/Shutterstock.com, (visitor's guide paper background) Andrey_Kuzmin/Shutterstock.com; cover, p. 1 (main) StompingGirl/Shutterstock.com; cover, p. 1 (inset) Nagel Photography/Shutterstock.com; pp. 5, 21 (Midwest map) LulaWanderwood/Shutterstock.com; p. 7 EquineEmily/Shutterstock.com, (inset) kavram/Shutterstock.com; p. 9 Eddie J. Rodriquez/Shutterstock.com; p. 11 Huntstyle/Shutterstock.com; p. 13 AevanStock/Shutterstock.com; p. 15 EWY Media/Shutterstock.com; p. 16 (arrows) Elina Li/Shutterstock.com; p. 17 (left) Zack Frank/Shutterstock.com; p. 17 (right) melissamn/Shutterstock.com; p. 19 Lena Platonova/Shutterstock.com.

All rights reserved. No part of this book may be reproduced in any form without permission in writing from the publisher, except by a reviewer.

Some of the images in this book illustrate individuals who are models. The depictions do not imply actual situations or events.

Printed in the United States of America

CPSIA compliance information: Batch #CWENS24: For further information contact Enslow Publishing at 1-800-398-2504.

CONTENTS

HOME IN THE HEARTLAND 4
JOINING THE UNITED STATES 6
THE MISSISSIPPI RIVER 8
WEATHER IN THE MIDWEST 10
CHICAGO, ILLINOIS 12
FAMOUS MIDWESTERNERS 14
NATIVE AMERICANS 16
THE BREADBASKET 18
GATEWAY ARCH 20
GLOSSARY 22
FOR MORE INFORMATION 23
INDEX 24

Words in the glossary appear in **bold** type the first time they are used in the text.

HOME IN THE HEARTLAND

Located in the northern center of the United States, the Midwest is a vast, or large, area. Sometimes called "America's heartland," the Midwest is important not just for its history but also for its countless farms growing food for America and other countries.

Today, the U.S. government considers the Midwest to include 12 states. These states each have their own features that make them great stops on a trip through the Midwest!

• **VISITOR'S GUIDE** •

TODAY, OVER 68 MILLION PEOPLE LIVE IN THE MIDWEST.

This map shows all the U.S. states that are part of the Midwest.

JOINING THE UNITED STATES

The Midwest became part of the United States in two pieces. The **Northwest Territory** was added to the country in the 1780s. The Great Plains were added as part of the **Louisiana Purchase** in 1803. The Great Plains are a huge area of grasslands covering the states of Kansas, Nebraska, North Dakota, and South Dakota and parts of other states.

The Badlands are part of South Dakota. Unlike the Great Plains, they grow very few plants! The Badlands are rocky with many **canyons**.

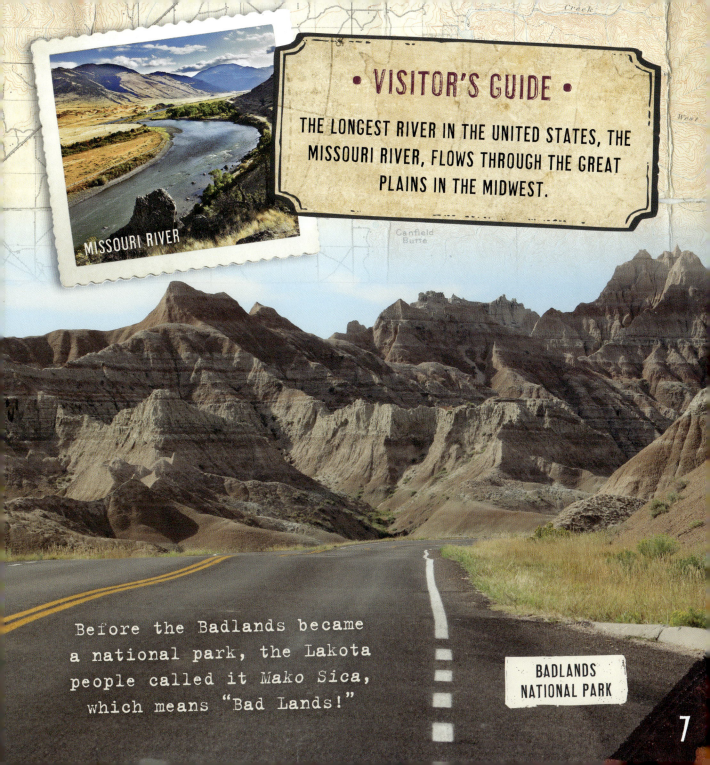

MISSOURI RIVER

• VISITOR'S GUIDE •

THE LONGEST RIVER IN THE UNITED STATES, THE MISSOURI RIVER, FLOWS THROUGH THE GREAT PLAINS IN THE MIDWEST.

Before the Badlands became a national park, the Lakota people called it *Mako Sica*, which means "Bad Lands!"

BADLANDS NATIONAL PARK

THE MISSISSIPPI RIVER

The Midwest is home to the upper part of the Mississippi River and four of the Great Lakes. This makes the Midwest great for fishing.

The Mississippi River starts at Lake Itasca in Park Rapids, Minnesota. In the Midwest, it serves as a natural border for Wisconsin, Iowa, Illinois, Missouri, and part of Minnesota. At Itasca State Park in Minnesota, the Mississippi River is narrow enough to cross on foot!

> Every year, boats carry around 175 million tons (158.7 mt) of goods on the Mississippi River.

MISSISSIPPI RIVER

• VISITOR'S GUIDE •

THE MISSISSIPPI AND MISSOURI RIVERS ARE VERY CLOSE IN LENGTH. THE MISSISSIPPI RIVER IS ABOUT 2,340 MILES LONG (3,765.8 KM) AND IS ABOUT 100 MILES (160.9 KM) SHORTER THAN THE MISSOURI RIVER!

WEATHER IN THE MIDWEST

The Midwest has a wide range of weather! This makes packing for a trip across the **region** a challenge. Summers can be very hot, but snow and ice are common in the winter. This weather can make roads slippery, and driving through the region can be dangerous during the winter!

Winter weather isn't the only thing to look out for in the Midwest. **Tornado** Alley is an area that has many tornadoes. Parts of Kansas, Missouri, Iowa, and Nebraska are in Tornado Alley.

• VISITOR'S GUIDE •

THERE CAN BE A 100-DEGREE TEMPERATURE DIFFERENCE BETWEEN THE HIGHS OF SUMMER AND THE LOWS OF WINTER IN SOME PLACES IN THE MIDWEST.

Iowa gets around 50 tornadoes each year.

CHICAGO, ILLINOIS

Many of the Midwest's major cities are connected by Interstate 90. These cities include Cleveland, Ohio; Gary, Indiana; and Chicago, Illinois.

Chicago is the third-largest city in the United States, with a population of about 2.7 million. It was the second-largest city in the country in 1890, only about 50 years after being founded! Today, Chicago has ballet companies, sports teams, and a famous silver **sculpture** sometimes called "The Bean" by visitors.

• VISITOR'S GUIDE •

VISITORS TO CHICAGO CAN ALSO ENJOY ONE OF CHICAGO'S FAMOUS DEEP-DISH PIZZAS OR A CHICAGO-STYLE HOT DOG!

The silver, bean-shaped piece of art in Chicago's Millennium Park is actually named Cloud Gate.

FAMOUS MIDWESTERNERS

Many famous Americans were born in the Midwest. There are historic sites and **museums** that honor people such as the Wright brothers and Walt Disney.

At the Mark Twain Boyhood Home and Museum in Hannibal, Missouri, visitors can learn all about the man who wrote *The Adventures of Tom Sawyer*. The Amelia Earhart Birthplace Museum in Atchison, Kansas, shares the life of the famous pilot before her flight disappeared in 1937.

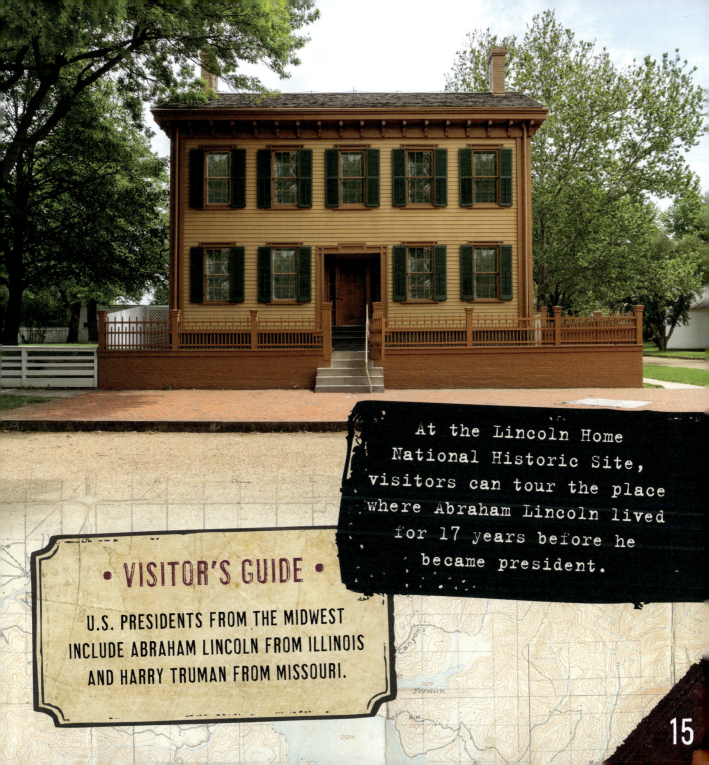

At the Lincoln Home National Historic Site, visitors can tour the place where Abraham Lincoln lived for 17 years before he became president.

• VISITOR'S GUIDE •

U.S. PRESIDENTS FROM THE MIDWEST INCLUDE ABRAHAM LINCOLN FROM ILLINOIS AND HARRY TRUMAN FROM MISSOURI.

NATIVE AMERICANS

Native American peoples lived in the Midwest before any settler set foot on the land. In fact, there are mounds of earth built by these peoples that date back thousands of years! The Effigy Mounds National Monument in Iowa allows visitors a close look at the site while learning about Native American history.

Many groups of Native Americans still live throughout the region. Today, people in these groups often continue the **traditions** of their people.

The mounds at the Effigy Mounds National Monument are believed to be burial spots.

• VISITOR'S GUIDE •

In South Dakota, artist Dale Lamphere created a 50-foot-tall (15 m) sculpture **dedicated** to the Native American people that live there. The statue is called *Dignity of Earth and Sky* and faces the Missouri River.

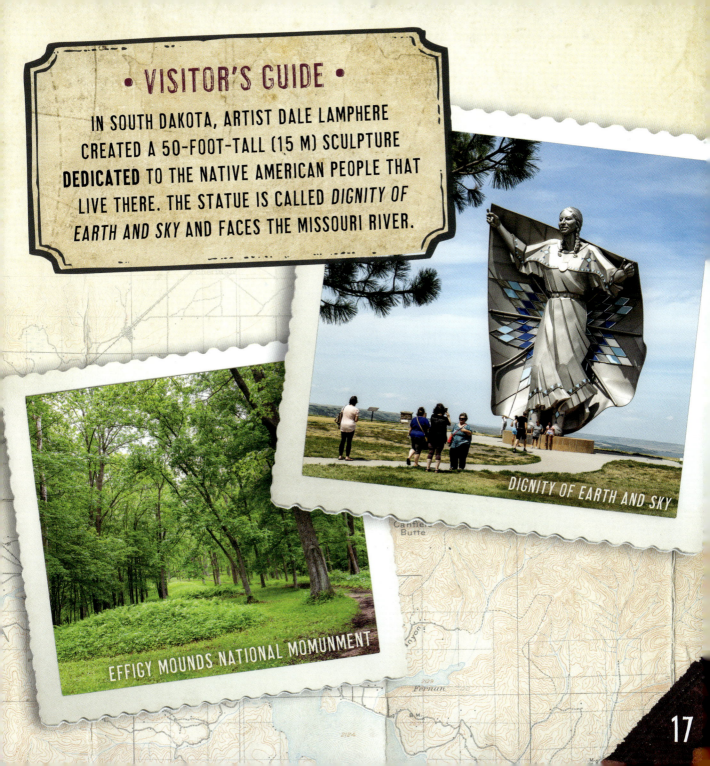

DIGNITY OF EARTH AND SKY

EFFIGY MOUNDS NATIONAL MOMUMENT

THE BREADBASKET

Some of the most productive farmland in the United States can be found in the Midwest. This includes parts of the Great Plains region. This area produces a lot of the top three farm **exports** in the United States! Farms producing soybeans, corn, and beef can be found throughout the Midwest.

Much of the United States' exported wheat is also grown on the Great Plains. In 2022, North Dakota produced the most wheat in the country.

• VISITOR'S GUIDE •

THE MIDWEST IS KNOWN FOR COMFORT FOODS THAT ARE OFTEN MADE WITH GRAINS GROWN ON THE GREAT PLAINS.

The Midwest is sometimes called the breadbasket of the United States.

GATEWAY ARCH

At Gateway **Arch** National Park in Missouri, visitors can see another famous Midwestern monument. The 630-foot (192 m) tall arch is the tallest monument in the United States. It was built in the 1960s to mark St. Louis, Missouri, as the starting point for earlier American expansion toward the West.

With so many states, each with their own history and things to explore and do, the Midwest has something for every visitor!

• VISITOR'S GUIDE •

THE GATEWAY ARCH WAS CREATED BY EERO SAARINEN, A FINNISH AMERICAN **ARCHITECT**. TODAY, VISITORS CAN TAKE A RIDE TO THE TOP OF THE GATEWAY ARCH!

MORE THINGS TO SEE IN THE MIDWEST

Check out more places to stop on your trip through the Midwest!

MOUNT RUSHMORE

Located in the Black Hills of South Dakota, visitors can see the 60-foot (18 m) tall faces of the U.S. presidents George Washington, Thomas Jefferson, Theodore Roosevelt, and Abraham Lincoln.

MALL OF AMERICA

Opened in 1992, the Mall of America in Bloomington, Minnesota, is the largest shopping mall in the United States.

THE CHILDREN'S MUSEUM OF INDIANAPOLIS

The largest children's museum in the world is found in Indianapolis, Indiana.

SAINT LOUIS ZOO

In Saint Louis, Missouri, the visitors to the zoo can get in for free!

21

GLOSSARY

arch: A structure built in the shape of a curve.

architect: A person who designs buildings.

canyon: A deep valley with steep sides.

dedicate: To honor a person, group, or event officially with something.

export: A good that is sold to another country.

Louisiana Purchase: The area between the Mississippi River and the Rocky Mountains that the U.S. government bought from France in 1803.

museum: A building in which things of interest are displayed.

Northwest Territory: Land east of the Mississippi River that the U.S. government gained after the American Revolution. It became Ohio, Michigan, Indiana, Illinois, Wisconsin, and a small part of Minnesota.

region: A large area of land that has features that make it different from nearby areas of land.

sculpture: A shape created with stone, wood, metal, or other matter.

tornado: A strong storm with winds that move in a funnel shape.

tradition: Custom practiced for a long time by certain cultures and people.

FOR MORE INFORMATION

Books

Holdren, Annie C. *Building the Gateway Arch.* Mankato, MN: Amicus, 2023.

Spanier, Kristine. *Explore the Midwest.* Minneapolis, MN: Pogo, 2023.

Websites

Britannica Kids: The Midwest
kids.britannica.com/kids/article/The-Midwest/489348
Learn more important facts about the Midwest.

National Geographic Kids: Illinois
www.kids.nationalgeographic.com/geography/states/article/Illinois
Learn more about the history of Illinois with interesting facts and pictures.

Publisher's note to educators and parents: Our editors have carefully reviewed these websites to ensure that they are suitable for students. Many websites change frequently, however, and we cannot guarantee that a site's future contents will continue to meet our high standards of quality and educational value. Be advised that students should be closely supervised whenever they access the internet.

INDEX

Badlands National Park, 6, 7

Effigy Mounds National Monument, 16, 17

Gateway Arch, 20

Illinois, 5, 8, 12, 13, 15, 21

Indiana, 5, 21

Iowa, 5, 8, 10, 11, 16, 21

Kansas, 5, 6, 10, 14, 21

Lake Itasca, 8

Lakota, 7

Lamphere, Dale, 17

Lincoln, Abraham, 15, 21

Michigan, 5, 21

Minnesota, 5, 8, 21

Mississippi River, 8, 9

Missouri, 5, 8, 10, 14, 15, 20, 21

Missouri River, 7, 17

Mount Rushmore, 21

Native Americans, 16, 17

Nebraska, 5, 6, 10, 21

North Dakota, 5, 6, 18

Ohio, 5, 21

South Dakota, 5, 6, 17, 21

Wisconsin, 5, 8, 21